Is God Really My Father?

By Dr. Connie Palm

Gospel Publishing Mission

P.O. Box 1065 ~ Hobe Sound, FL 33475
www.gospelpublishingmission.org
A ministry of *Hope International Missions*

Published by Gospel Publishing Mission, a ministry of
Hope International Missions

by Dr. Connie Palm

Illustrated by Richard & Francis Hook, except pages 5&7

Layout and cover design by Robert Scott/Clear Graphics

Contents

Important Note

International English is a very easy-to-read vocabulary of about 1,500 basic English words. This is especially helpful to young readers and for those who speak English as a second language.

There are times when words must be used which are not in the group of words that makes up International English. The meaning of these words is given in the glossary at the back of this book. The first time these words are used they have a special marking like this: sword^G. When you see a word marked with a ^{G} like this, look in the glossary for the meaning.

Heaven

God has a home for us. 1 Corinthians 2:9

There is a place called heaven. Heaven is God's home. He wants it to be your home also. Let me tell you about this place.

Heaven is peaceful. In heaven, people do not argue or fight. They do not hurt each other with words. No one steals your things. No one lies about you.

Heaven is full of joy and happiness. Smiles and laughter are everywhere. It never gets dark in heaven. No one has a hurting heart. No one is hopeless, or sad, without food or friends.

Here are some things you never hear in heaven:
"You do not belong."
"You are not good enough."
"I hate you."

Here are some things you do hear in heaven:
"I love you."
"You are family."
"You are accepted just as you are."

In heaven there is no crying alone at night. There is no crying because you failed or are afraid. God takes away all your tears.

Are you ever sick? In heaven, all sickness and pain are gone. No one dies. You can be in this safe, happy place forever.

There are beautiful living spaces in heaven. You will not be lonely! There are people from all over the world. There are people who speak every language. There are people from every race and of every color.

This home is made by God, our Heavenly Father; and Jesus, His Son; and the Holy Spirit, Who is our Guide. These three are called the Trinity. Trinity means the Three-in-One God: Father, Son and Holy Spirit.

Heaven is made for every child of God. Are you God's child?

If you say, "No" or "I don't know" please go on reading. This book explains how you can become God's child. It explains how you can live in heaven forever when you leave this world.

Angels, Good and Bad

We have an enemy. Genesis 3, Jude 6, Isaiah 14:12

God is not alone in heaven. Long, long ago, longer ago than you can imagine, God created angels[G] to be with Him. Angels are God's helpers. Angels kneel down to worship God. They listen to God and obey Him.

Angels are not like people. Angels are beings who do not have bodies. But they are able to do their work by using a body when they need to. Angels have great power but they do not have as much power as God has.

When angels were created they had no sin. They were beautiful. The most beautiful of all the angels was one named Lucifer. The name "Lucifer" means "the morning star–the one who carries light."

When Lucifer was created, he was not only perfect in beauty but also full of wisdom. God gave Lucifer a high position. He was the head leader over many angels.

Lucifer's great beauty made him proud. This sin of pride came from inside himself.

Lucifer began to think, "I am very wise. Perhaps I am as wise as God. I have power. Many angels do as I say. Perhaps my power is as great as God's power. My beauty is great. Perhaps I can have anything I want."

What Lucifer wanted was to be like God. He wanted to be Number One. He wanted to sit in God's place. Little by little, Lucifer talked to other angels. "Come, join me. I will be like God. If you follow me, you will not be sorry. You will have great gain." About one-third of the angels joined Lucifer. They rebelled against God.

And so there was war in heaven. The good angels, who obeyed and worshiped God, fought with the bad angels, who followed Lucifer. Lucifer lost the battle. He and all the angels who followed him were thrown out of heaven.

To punish Lucifer and the bad angels, God made a special place called "hell." Hell is the opposite of heaven. It is the place of terrible punishment and death that never ends.

Lucifer's name was changed. Now he is called Satan or the devil. From that day until now, Satan has been the enemy of God.

Good angels still obey and worship God.

Creation
God's first plan begin. He made us to be His friend.
Genesis 1&2

God has no birthday. He has always existed. In the beginning there was no world at all. There was no light. God decided to make the heavens and the earth. God spoke and all was created.

God said, "Let there be light!" and there was light. He spoke and the sky, land and sea were made. God had only to speak and trees and plants came out of the earth. He spoke, and the sun, moon and stars came into being. God spoke, and fish filled the oceans and rivers. The brightly colored birds filled the sky. God spoke and the animals, large and small, were created.

"Now," God said , "I will create the best of all. I will make a man. Man will be very different from all the animals. I will make him a little like myself. He will be able to love. He will be able to think and speak. He will be able to choose for himself what he will do and he will be responsible for the choices he makes. I have a special purpose for man. I want him to love Me and talk to Me and be My son."

So God took some earth and made it into the shape of a man. God gave this shape His own breath. Man became a living person with a soul. This soul is the part of man that lives forever. God called the man "Adam."

God saw that it was not good for Adam to be alone. God said, "I will make someone to help him." While Adam was sleeping, God removed a bone from Adam's side and made a beautiful woman from it. Adam called her "Eve."

God wanted Adam to have a place to live, so He planted a beautiful garden called Eden. It had many trees, plants and flowers.

Adam and Eve, son and daughter of God, were very happy. In the beautiful place God had made for them, they had everything they needed. The best time of every day was when they talked to God.

God made only one rule. Adam and Eve were to show their love for God by always obeying this rule. God looked at all He had created and said, "It is good."

But...something happened. shame. They talked with God every day.

Sin

Adam and Eve enjoyed their beautiful garden home. They listened to the birds. They played with the animals. They smelled the flowers. They did not wear clothes because they were without

God had said, "There is only one thing you must not do. You must not eat the fruit that grows on one tree. It is the tree in the center of the garden. It is the tree that gives the power to know Right and Wrong. If you do, everything will change and one day you will die. If you love Me, you must choose to obey."

God's enemy, Satan, wants to destroy everything God loves. One day Satan took the shape of a snake. He found Eve walking alone and said, "Did God really say you must not eat any of the fruit here?"

"No, God did not say that," said Eve. "We can eat every fruit except one. If we eat that one, we will die some day."

"That is not true," said Satan. "You will not die. No! You will become like God. See, the fruit is wonderful! Eat it!"

The fruit did look good. Why not eat just a little? Eve ate the fruit and ran to give some to Adam. He ate it. What a terrible choice they made!

Immediately they knew that they had sinned. They were ashamed that they were naked. They were afraid to talk to God.

Not obeying brought many bad things into the world: pain, sickness, hate and hurts of all kinds. For all time every child would be born with the desire to sin.

God's heart was broken. He loved Adam and Eve but they must be punished. He took the lives of animals and with their skins He made good clothes for Adam and Eve. This covering showed them that God would provide for them and protect them.

The clothes that were made when animals gave their life and their blood was a picture of what Jesus, God's Son, would do many, many years later. Jesus gave His life and His blood to make a covering for our sins. But we must believe that Jesus did that for us. We must repent and turn from our sins. If we will do that, we can have life forever in heaven.

Adam and Eve had to leave their beautiful home. God put angels^G at the gate with a shining sword^G. Adam and Eve could never go back.

Satan destroyed God's first plan. But God promised to send His Son. His Son would one day destroy Satan. So God began a new plan to find people who would love and obey Him. You are a part of this plan. God has a purpose for you!

The Huge Boat
God has made a safe place for all who obey Him.
Genesis 6-9

As time went on, more and more people lived in the world but they all forgot God. People became evil, selfish^G and cruel.

Wait! There was one man named Noah. Noah and his family were the only ones who loved and obeyed God.

"I need your help," Noah said to his three sons. "God has told me to build a huge boat. It must be big enough to carry a male and female of every kind of animal."

"That would be a very big boat! Why must you build it?" asked Noah's sons.

"God has told me that He will send a flood to destroy the world and all the people in it because they are so evil. I believe what God says. Will you help me?"

"Yes, Father, we will help."

Noah and his sons started to work. People came to watch. "Noah, you are a fool," they said. "There has never been a flood. How will this huge boat float?"

Year after year, as Noah worked, he told the people to repent. Punishment was coming. All would be destroyed. No one believed him.

One day everything was ready. The animals were all in the boat. Noah and his family went inside. God shut the door. Then the rain came. Water poured from the sky. Now the people believed Noah. They begged to be let inside, but it was too late.

It rained forty days and nights. Noah said to his family, "Outside there are death and danger. The people are punished for their sins and unbelief. We are safe in the boat. Because we believe what He says, God will not punish us."

After many months the huge boat came to rest on a mountain. Noah and his family came out into a fresh, washed world. They gave thanks to God.

"Look, Father, what is that beautiful thing in the sky? It is made of bright, happy colors." It was a rainbow^G.

God made a promise, "Never again will I send a flood to destroy the world. When you see a rainbow, remember My promise."

Today God tells us, "If you believe what I say and love and obey Me, you will be in a safe place. I will watch over you and bring you to your home in heaven."

God's Plan
The blood on the door is a picture of God's <u>best plan</u>. Exodus 11-12

Years and years and years went by. Many wonderful things happened.

God called Abraham to be the father of a nation of people. God explained His plan to Abraham. God said, "I will teach the people of this nation to love and serve Me. One day My Son, Jesus, will be born into this nation. Jesus will make a way for everyone in the world to have eternal life. Everyone has sinned. The punishment for sin is death. Without the giving of blood, sin cannot be forgiven. The blood of animals is not good enough. Every sinner should be punished for his own sins. But Jesus will take the place of all sinners and will die in their place. If any sinner is sorry for his sin and trusts that Jesus died in his place, he will be saved from never-ending death and will have never-ending life."

Little by little, God's wonderful plan began to happen just as He said it would. God gave Abraham a son named Isaac. Isaac's son was Jacob. Jacob had a son named Joseph. Joseph was sold to be a slave in Egypt. God was with Joseph and he became a ruler in Egypt.

The people of God grew and grew in number. After Joseph died, that number continued to grow. The Egyptians were afraid of God's people and made them slaves.

God spoke to a man named Moses and said, "Moses you must take My people out of Egypt to a land I promise to give them."

The king refused to let them go. God caused nine terrible things to happen to Egypt. The king still said, "No!"

Then Moses said to the king, "Tonight God will pass over this land. The first-born person in every family will die."

Moses told God's people what would happen. Then he said, "Take a perfect lamb[G] and kill it. Put its blood on top of your door and on each side of the door. When God sees the blood, He will pass by and you will be safe." God's people obeyed and no harm came to them. But in the houses of Egypt every first-born was dead.

This was called the Passover. After the Passover, the king said to Moses, "Go! Do not come back!" Moses and God's people started the long trip to their new land. And what a trip they had!

The meaning of Passover became clear when Jesus came into the world. Jesus, the perfect Lamb of God, gave His blood for us. Ask Him to cover your sins with His blood. Then you will receive mercy from God. You will escape the punishment of never-ending death.

Ten Good Rules

God shows you how to live "inside" and "outside" so you will "fit" in heaven. Exodus 20

Moses and God's people traveled toward their new land. They came to the Red Sea. They did not know that the King of Egypt had changed his mind. He sent his army to bring God's people back to Egypt.

God's people said, "Look! There comes the army behind us! Look! There is the Red Sea in front of us! What will we do?"

God said, "I will rescue you!" God opened a path through the Red Sea. His people walked across on dry ground. When the army of Egypt followed, God made the water close on them and they drowned.

God went with His people. When they were thirsty, God gave them water. When they were hungry, God gave them food.

Three months went by. God's people came to a mountain called Sinai. God said to Moses, "Now it is time to give My people some rules to live by. These rules will help them love Me and will help them live together. If My people will obey My voice and keep My rules, I will lead them and take care of them."

Moses went up the mountain. The people heard thunder^G. They saw lightning. God gave Moses two flat pieces of stone. The Ten Rules were written on the stones. God wrote with His finger and here is what He wrote:

1. Worship Me only. Do not worship anyone or anything else.
2. Do not make any idol^G, or picture or image to worship.
3. My name is holy. Speak My name with respect^G.
4. Do your work in six days. Keep day number seven for Me.
5. Honor your father and mother.
6. Do not murder.
7. Do not break the promises you make when you marry.
8. Do not steal.
9. Do not lie.
10. Do not let your heart desire anything that belongs to another person.

Moses came down from the mountain. He carried the words of God written on the stones. He saw that the people were frightened. "Do

not be afraid," he said. "God gave you these rules because He loves you. He wants you to know how to please Him and be happy in this life and in heaven."

The people said, "We will do what God says." Do you think they kept this promise?

The Fierce Snakes
You must believe Jesus exists and that He died for you.
Numbers 21:4-9

God's people traveled in the desert on their way to the land God had promised them. They were hot, tired and unhappy. Their feet hurt. They did not like the food. They spoke against God. They spoke against Moses. They said, "This trip is so difficult! We wish we were back in Egypt!"

God was very angry. He sent fierce snakes into their camp[G]. The snakes were all over the place. They bit many of the people. People were dying. The people knew they had sinned. They went to Moses for help. "Moses, please pray for us. Ask God to take away these terrible snakes."

Moses prayed. God did not take away the snakes, but He told Moses what to do. God said, "I will give you a cure for the bite of the snake. Make a snake out of metal and put it on a very high pole[G]. Put the snake where every person can see it. Look and live! If anyone will look and will have faith in God's cure for his sin, that person will not die." Moses might have thought that was an unusual way to solve the problem, but he obeyed God.

Some of the people who had been bitten did not want to believe that this would work. Let us listen to their excuses.

"That's an insane idea."
"That's too easy."
"That's impossible."
"I can save myself."
"I will wait until later."

These all died. But every person who looked at the cure God had given and believed what God said did not die. The snake was teaching about Jesus Who would come into the world many years later.

Jesus would die on a cross that was lifted up where every person could see. All of us have sinned. All of us need a Saviour. Jesus is that Saviour. We must believe and not make excuses.

Jesus Will Come
God promised, in detail, the coming and sacrifice of His Son.
Isaiah 7:14, Isaiah 53, Micah 5:2

One day the long trip from Egypt to the land God had promised was over. God's people built homes and planted gardens. They had children. They had leaders and they made laws. They built a house in which to worship God. They still used the blood of animals as a sacrifice for sin.

Over hundreds of years, God kept on telling them that He would send His Son, Jesus, into the world when the time was right. God often spoke to His special leaders. He told them many details about the coming of Jesus and about His life and death.

Isaiah was one of those special leaders. This is what he said about Jesus. "He will be hated and will be a man of suffering. He will take upon Himself our troubles and carry our sorrows. He will be crushed for our sins. He will be punished so that we can have peace.

"All of us like sheep^G have gone the wrong way. Each of us has turned to his own way. And God has put on Jesus the sin of us all. He will be taken like a lamb^G and be put to death. He will be hurt because of the sin of the people who should have been punished."

God told them that Jesus would be born in Bethlehem. He said Jesus would be born of a woman who had never had a man. Jesus would be betrayed for thirty pieces of silver. He would die on a cross. God said, "When Jesus dies, not one bone of His body will be broken." God said that Jesus would be raised from the dead.

Was Jesus really coming? Would God keep His promise? Would it happen exactly as God said?

Many people forgot the words of God. They thought only about money and how to become rich. They thought about good food and having fun. They thought about how to get power and how to get high position.

But there were always a few who remembered God's words. They believed what God said. They waited and waited until one day....

Jesus Is Born
God's <u>best</u> plan begins. Luke 2

God said, "The right time has come. My Son, Who has always been with Me, will now begin His life on earth."

God sent an angel^G to a young woman named Mary. "Do not be afraid, Mary. You are honored very much. God has chosen you. You will become a mother and have a Son. You must call Him Jesus."

Mary said, "How can this happen? I have never had a man."

The angel said, "The power of God will cover you. God will make the baby grow inside you. This Holy Child is God's own Son. He is the One God promised to Adam and Eve and to God's special helpers. He will be the sacrifice for every person's sin."

Mary said, "I am willing. Let it happen to me as you have said."

Mary had promised to be the wife of a good man named Joseph. Mary told him what had happened. Joseph was troubled. God came to Joseph in a dream. "Joseph, it is just as Mary has said. Do not be afraid to marry her."

This was wonderful. God Himself was the Father of Mary's baby. Joseph married Mary and took gentle care of her.

The king of the land said every man must go to the place of his birth and be counted. Joseph had to go to Bethlehem and took Mary with him. The baby would be born soon. The trip was long. Mary was tired. In Bethlehem, they could not find a room.

One kind man said, "You can stay in the place where my animals sleep. It is warm. You can be alone."

That very night God's Son was born. Mary laid Jesus in the box where the cattle were fed.

Not far away shepherds^G were watching their sheep^G. They had a great surprise! A bright light appeared. An angel said, "I bring you good news of great joy. Tonight Jesus is born! Go and see for yourselves!" The shepherds found Jesus. They knew He was the One Who had been promised. How happy they were!

Far, far away a special star came into the sky. Three wise men knew its meaning. The Saviour was born! They traveled a long time. When they found Jesus, they gave Him gold and rich gifts.

God kept His promise. His plan began on time!

Nicodemus
Jesus wants your heart and life to become new. John 3:1-21

Jesus grew strong and tall. He helped His father and mother. He obeyed them. When Jesus was thirty years old, He began to tell people about God's plan. Some people believed He was the Son of God. Other people hated Him.

A man named Nicodemus went to talk to Jesus at night. He wanted to know how to go to heaven. Jesus said, "You cannot go to heaven unless you are born again."

"Teacher, how can that be?" Nicodemus asked. "How can a man get into his mother's body and be born the second time?"

Jesus said, "A baby has a body like his parents when he is born. God has no body. He is Spirit. It is in your heart, not your body, that you are born again. God gives you a new heart."

"But how?" asked Nicodemus.

Jesus said, "Do you feel the wind that is blowing? Do you see how it moves the leaves on the trees? You know the wind is blowing. You can feel it. You can see what it does, but you do not know how the wind blows.

"In the same way when your soul is born again by the power of God, you know it has happened but not how it happened."

"How is this possible?" asked Nicodemus.

Jesus said, "Soon the people who hate Me will put Me to death on a cross. Do you remember how Moses lifted up the snake? The people did not die if they believed God would save them. Any person who believes I die in his place will have all sin taken away. He will have a clean, new-born heart. He can go to heaven." Nicodemus believed what Jesus said.

God loves us so much. He gave His only Son to die in our place. If you believe, your sins will be forgiven and you will have life that lasts forever.

Jesus wants you to have a new-born heart and new life. Do you believe Jesus died for you? Will you accept His gift of a new heart and a new life?

How to Live

After you are new-born, Jesus wants you to have certain behavior.
Matthew 5-6

After you are new-born, God wants you to have actions that please Him. Jesus taught us how to please God.

It was a beautiful day. People hurried to the hill where Jesus was talking. They sat on the ground and listened carefully.

Jesus said:

"Give up everything that would keep you from loving God with all your heart.

"Be as obedient and as believing as a little child.

"Trust God, your Heavenly Father, for all the things you need. Do not worry.

"You know the Ten Rules given to Moses. You must go beyond these rules. Do not pay back wrong for wrong.

"Love your enemy. Help your enemy and pray for him. You must forgive in the way God does. Do not hold hate in your heart.

"Do not criticize others. Do not want to be first. Be happy to give to others.

"Act toward other people the same way you want them to act toward you."

The people listened and thought, "This is not easy. Can a person really live like this?"

Jesus knew their thoughts. He said, "Ask God to help you live like this. He loves you. He knows you cannot live like this by your own power. He will give you the power to live as you should. He will help you, for sure!"

Today, God will help you in the same way!

A Boy and His Lunch

Jesus can do anything, but He wants your help. John 6:1-14

More and more people wanted to hear Jesus talk. One day a boy asked, "Mother, may I go to listen to Jesus?"

"Yes," his mother said. "You will have to walk a long way. You will be hungry. You must take a lunch." She gave him five little loaves^G of bread and two small fish in a bag. "Go, and be careful," his mother said.

The boy walked a long way.   He arrived at the place where Jesus was teaching. More than 5,000 people were already there. The boy was so excited that he did not take time to eat.

The hours went by. The people had eaten all the food they had brought. Now they were very hungry.

Jesus said to His helpers, "We must feed the people."

His helpers said, "There is no place to buy bread here in the desert. If bread could be bought, we have no money."

Jesus said, "You can give them food to eat."

"It is impossible," His helpers said. " We don't have one bit of food."

The boy with the lunch heard about the problem. He went to Jesus' helpers and said, "I have five little loaves of bread and two small fish. That is not much food but I will give it all to you."

Jesus smiled and took the lunch. He told all the people to sit down. He prayed to His Father in heaven. Jesus broke the bread and fish into pieces. The more He broke the more there was!

The helpers gave the food to all the people. They had all they wanted to eat. There was a lot of extra food.

Jesus may have said to the boy, "You gave Me all you had and God's power made it enough for all the people. You made God happy. You made others happy. You did not think of yourself only. You may take some of the extra food home with you."

The boy may have said, "It is good to give all to God. Now I am the most happy of all!"

God can do anything, but sometimes He wants your help. Give Him all you have. God will bless you and will make you a blessing to others.

The Good Neighbor

Jesus wants you to love Him and also love others as much as you love yourself. Luke 10:30-37

One day a man asked Jesus, "What must I do to go to heaven?"

The answer was, "You must love God with all your heart. You must love your neighbor as you love yourself."

"Who is my neighbor?" the man asked. Jesus told a story to answer the question.

There were two groups of people who hated each other. One group was called Jews. The other group was called Samaritans.

One day a Jew was traveling a lonely road from one town to another. He should not have traveled alone. It was a dangerous road. Suddenly robbers^G jumped out and attacked him. They stole his money and his clothes. The robbers beat him and left him almost dead.

It happened that an important Jew was going down that same road. He saw the poor man but he would not stop to help. He went by on the other side of the road. Later another Jew came by. He was in a hurry. He passed by, also. These two refused to help a man of their own group.

Soon a man from Samaria came down the road riding on a donkey^G. He saw the Jew and had mercy on him. He stopped to help. The Samaritan put oil and wine where the man was cut. He tied up the wounds of the hurt Jew.

The Samaritan put the man on his own donkey. They went to a place where people stay for the night. The Samaritan stayed all through the night and took care of the Jew.

The next day the Samaritan had to leave. He said to the owner of the resting place, "Here is money. Take care of this man. I will come back. If you need more money than this, I will give it to you when I come again."

Three people saw the hurt man. Which one had mercy? Which one showed love? Which one helped? Which one was a good neighbor?

Our neighbor is the person who needs our help, whoever he is. Jesus wants us to be kind to everyone.

The Good Shepherd

Jesus does not want even one person to be lost. **John 10:1-21**

Jesus said, "I am like a shepherd^G Who takes good care of the sheep^G. Those who follow Me are My sheep. I know each one by name. I give My life for the sheep."

Jesus told this story. Once there was a shepherd who had 100 sheep. He loved each one of them. He always counted his sheep at the end of the day to be sure that they were all there. One night he counted–97, 98, 99. He discovered that one sheep was missing.

The shepherd left the 99 sheep in a safe place. He went to look for the one lost sheep. It was dark. There were wild animals. There was danger. The shepherd searched and searched. He did not give up. After a long time, he heard the sheep. It was tired and hurt. It was caught in the sharp thorns^G. It was crying for help. The shepherd reached far down to rescue the sheep. The shepherd put the lost sheep on his shoulder and carried it home.

There are millions of people in the world. Our heavenly Father loves each one. You are important to God. He knows where you live. He knows your name. He cares for you as if you were the only person in all the world.

Are you a lost sheep? We are all lost sheep because all of us have done bad things. We have wandered away from God. God sent His Son to search for each one of us to save us from the punishment of sin.

Do you think, "I have gone too far away, I have fallen down too deep into sin, Jesus cannot help me"? That is not true! Call to Him and He will answer you.

He is the Good Shepherd Who gave His life for you. He will save you. He will lift you up. He will guide you and protect you. He will lead you to safety in His Father's house.

The Lost Son

No matter how bad you are, Jesus wants you to come back to Him.
Luke 15:11-32

One day many people came to hear Jesus talk. He told them a story about a rich man who had two sons.

The younger son wanted excitement and fun. "Father," he said, "I want my share of the money you are saving for my brother and me. I want it now." The son would not stop asking. The father was sad, but finally he gave him the money.

The son took the money and went far, far away. There he spent all he had on wild and foolish living. When he had no more money, his false friends left him. His clothes were torn and dirty. His stomach was empty.

The son got a job feeding pigs. He was so hungry he wanted to eat the pigs' food. One day, as he sat with the pigs, he thought, "In my father's house there is plenty of food and all I need. How foolish I was to leave my father. I am so ashamed, but I will get up and go back home and say, 'Father, I have sinned. I am not good enough to be your son. May I be one of the workers you pay?'"

The son started the long walk back to his father's house. Every step of the way he thought, "I wonder if Father will take me back?"

All this time the father waited and hoped for his son to return. Every day he stood by the door and watched for him. One day, in the distance, the father saw his son coming.

The father ran with his arms held out to his son. He hugged him close and kissed him. "Father, I have sinned against God and you. I only ask to be one of your..."

The father hugged him closer. "Hurry!" the father said to a worker. "Bring my son the best of everything. Prepare a feast. Let us eat and be full of joy. My son was dead and now he is alive again. He was lost and now he is found. He was far away but now he has come home."

Does God really keep on loving us if we rebel and go away from Him? Yes, He is like the father in this story. God is waiting with His arms held out for us to come back to Him. When we do, God welcomes us. He reminds us that His love for us will never change or go away.

The Little Man

Jesus loves you <u>where</u> you are and <u>how</u> you are. Luke 19:1-10

In Jericho there lived a man named Zacchaeus. He collected taxes. He was rich, but he had no friends. He often charged more tax than was right and kept the extra money for himself. He was not honest and no one wanted to be seen talking to him. His looks were against him, too. People made fun of him because he was so short.

Zacchaeus had heard about Jesus. More than anything, Zacchaeus wanted to talk to this wonderful Man Who was good and kind. But he had no hope of ever doing this. He was sure Jesus would never take time to visit with him.

One day the people on the street were talking. "Have you heard? Jesus is coming this way!"

"Here is my chance," thought Zacchaeus. "I know I cannot talk to Him, but at least I can see Him."

But the crowd was so large and Zacchaeus was so small that it was impossible to see. Zacchaeus did not give up. He quickly ran ahead of the crowd and climbed a tree. He thought, "This is perfect! I can see everybody but nobody can see me!"

The crowd came down the street. Jesus stopped beneath the very tree where Zacchaeus was. Jesus looked up into the tree and said, "Zacchaeus, you can come down now. I want to go to your house today."

Zacchaeus was so excited he nearly fell out of the tree. Jesus knew his name! Jesus knew what he was like and He still wanted to be his Friend. Zacchaeus was so happy. He took Jesus to his house and prepared a feast for Him.

The meeting with Jesus completely changed Zacchaeus' life. He said, "Jesus, I have done wrong. Now I want to be honest. I will give to the poor. I have cheated people. Now I will give them four times more than I took."

Jesus said, "Today salvation has come to this house. Man looks on the outside, but My Father looks on the inside and knows those who want to follow Him."

God accepts you where you are and how you are.

Jesus Died for Us
Jesus paid the price for your sin. Luke 22-23

The common people loved Jesus and followed Him. This made the rulers very angry and full of hate. They wanted to kill Jesus. Jesus knew the time had come for Him to finish God's plan. It was time for Him to die on the cross.

Jesus ate one last supper with His twelve special followers. Then they went to a lonely garden. There Jesus prayed, "My Father, if it is possible, save Me from this terrible death. But if this is what I must do, I am willing. I want to obey You."

Jesus was taken before Pilate, the ruler of the land. A large crowd of people, led by the enemies of Jesus, gathered together. Pilate talked to Jesus. Then he told the people, "I can find no wrong in Jesus. I want to release Him."

But all the crowd screamed, "Nail[G] Him to a cross! Nail Him to a cross!"

Pilate gave Jesus to the soldiers to be nailed to a cross. They beat Jesus. They made fun of Him and spit on Him. They put a crown of thorns[G] on His head and made Him carry His own cross. When they came to the place called Calvary, they nailed Jesus to a cross. He was lifted up and His blood flowed down.

Jesus prayed, "Father, forgive them." Then Jesus said, "I have finished what I came to do." And He died.

But that is not the end of the story!!

Here is the reason Jesus had to die. God is holy and hates sin. Sin always hurts and destroys the people God created. When Adam and Eve disobeyed God, they sinned. But God loves sinners and wants to save them from sin and death.

Before Jesus came, God told the people they could bring certain animals to the place of worship and offer them as a sacrifice for their sins so that they would not have to die. But this was not the perfect sacrifice. It had to be given over and over.

When Jesus came, He died for us. God did away with the Old Way and made a New Way. Now we do not have to offer other sacrifices. Jesus gave His blood once for all people for all time. Jesus took on Himself the punishment for sin that should have been given to the sinner.

When you believe this and put yourself in the care of Jesus, you become God's child. You are given eternal life.

Jesus Is Alive!
He lives, so you can have eternal life, too. Luke 24

There was a good man named Joseph. He went to Pilate and asked for the body of Jesus. He took the body down from the cross and put it in good cloth. He laid Jesus in a place that had been cut out in the side of a rock. A huge stone was put across the opening. The enemies of Jesus put soldiers to guard the place.

The friends of Jesus were so sad. Jesus was gone and their hearts were broken. The future was very dark. They had no hope of ever seeing Jesus again.

It was early Sunday morning three days after Jesus had died. Suddenly there was a strong earthquake. An angel[G] came down and rolled away the stone. Jesus came out! The soldiers who were on guard were so afraid that they fell to the ground. Then they ran away to tell what had happened.

Some women were going back to look at the place where the body of Jesus was laid. When the women got to the place where Jesus had been buried, the angel said, "Do not be afraid. You are looking for Jesus Who was nailed[G] to a cross. He is not here. He is risen! Come and see, then go and tell His followers the Good News!"

The women ran quickly. Could this really be true? Suddenly, Jesus met them and spoke to them. They fell at His feet and worshiped Him. Then the women returned to tell the other followers what they had seen.

The followers heard the women say, "Jesus is not dead! He is risen! We have seen Him! He lives!" Those who believed this were unspeakably happy. They knew that because Jesus was alive they also had hope and a future.

Jesus says to us, "Because I live, you will live also. I am the One Who raises the dead and gives them life. Anyone who puts his trust in Me will live again even if he dies."

Jesus Returns to Heaven

Jesus sent His Holy Spirit to live in your heart to help you live in a way that makes Jesus happy. 1 Corinthians 15:1-8

Jesus stayed on earth for forty days. He was seen many times after He arose from the dead. Once, more than 500 people saw Him at the same place.

Still, some followers doubted that Jesus was alive. One day, He came to some of them and said, "Why do you doubt? Look at My hands and My feet. See the marks of the nails^G that held Me on the cross. Touch Me. It is I, and I am alive." They touched and they believed.

Thomas was not there that day so his friends told him, "We have seen Jesus." He said, "I will not believe until I see the marks of the nails with my own eyes and put my own finger in them."

Eight days later, Jesus appeared to Thomas. "Thomas, touch the marks in My hands. Do not doubt, believe!"

Thomas knew it was Jesus and said to Him, "My Lord and my God!"

Jesus said, "Thomas, because you have seen Me, you believe. Blessed are those who have not seen Me and still believe."

After forty days Jesus went outside the town. A large crowd went with Him. Jesus lifted His hands and blessed them. He said, "Now I go to the Father. The Good News will be told in all the world. Then I will come back in power and shining brightness with all the holy angels^G. I will gather My people to Me forever. Be ready and hold to your faith in Me until I come." Jesus started to go up from the earth. He went up until He could no longer be seen.

Jesus promised that He would send the Holy Spirit to be with His followers. The Holy Spirit would be in the heart of every believer to give comfort and to guide and to help the believer to please God.

Jesus is now with God. Jesus prays for us and watches over us. When the time is right, Jesus will come back to earth again. The Christian dead will come out of their graves. Believers who are alive will rise up to meet Jesus. We will go to heaven. God's plan will be complete. What a wonderful day that will be!

Choosing to Belong

Jesus welcomes you and wants you to be a child of God.
Mark 10:13-16

Even before the world was made, God chose you for Himself because of His love. God planned for you to be His child. He made heaven for you. But it is not enough to say, "Let me in."

There are some things you must do:

You must believe that God exists.

You must have faith in God. Faith is believing that what God says is true. Do you believe what God says?

You must be sorry for your sins and turn from them. You must tell your sins to God. If you are sorry and tell Him your sins, you can depend on Him to forgive them. Are you sorry you have sinned?

You must trust Jesus. This means to put yourself in His care and not worry. He loves you. He accepts you. He keeps His promises.

Jesus made heaven possible for us when He gave His own blood as a gift to God. You have a choice. You can accept or reject this gift that Jesus offers you.

Please accept this gift. You will always be glad you did. You will belong to the family of God. You will go to heaven when you die. You will not go to the place prepared for Satan and his followers. Will you open your heart and ask Jesus to come in?

You can pray to God in your own way. He knows what your heart says. Or you can pray this prayer:

"God, I know that You exist and that You love me. I want to be Your child. I have sinned. I have ....(you can tell God all the sins you remember doing). I am sorry I have disobeyed You and have hurt others. Please forgive me. I open the door of my heart and ask You to come in right now. I trust You to accept me. I believe You do take my sins away. Thank You, Father. I love You. Help me to live for You and to learn more about You. I ask You to do this for me because Jesus gave His blood for me. Amen"

Tell Others

Jesus wants you to tell others what you know about Him.
Luke 5:1-11

Now you are God's child. At one time you did not belong to Him. Your mind was at war with Him. Your thoughts and actions were wrong. But Jesus has brought you to God by His death on the cross. Now you have life that will never end. This is good news that you can share with others.

One bright day Jesus was walking on the beach talking to people. The people pushed closer and closer. Jesus got into Peter's boat and asked him to go out a little way from the beach. Jesus talked to them from the boat.

When Jesus finished talking, He told Peter to go out into the deep water. "Now, Peter, let down your net^G and catch fish."

Peter said, "We fished all last night and did not catch one fish. I think there are no fish here. But I will do as You say."

What a surprise! The net came up with so many fish in it that the boat was about to sink! Peter had to call for help. The men who helped were Andrew, James and John. Jesus said to them, "Come follow Me. From now on I want you to fish for men."

Jesus meant that He wanted them to be His helpers. He wanted them to tell many people the good news about God's love.

Jesus wants you to be His helper. You can talk to your friends, your family and your neighbors. You can spread the Good News near and far. When people hear the truth, they can choose to go to heaven, too. Jesus wants us to bring others to heaven with us.

Jesus said, "You are to go to all the world and preach the Good News to every person. Teach them to do all the things I have told you. And I am with you always, even to the end of the world."

Will you tell others what you know about Jesus and God's good plan? Will you tell others what God has done for you?

Glossary

Angel: 1. A messenger of God. 2. A supernatural being, either good or bad.

Camp: A living place used for a short time.

Donkey: A horse-like animal with large ears.

Idol: An object to worship, a god.

Lamb: A young sheep.

Loaves: Bread baked in one piece.

Nail: A thin, round piece of metal used to hold things in place.

Net: Loosely knotted or woven string often used to catch fish or birds.

Pole: A long thin piece, usually of rounded wood.

Rainbow: A circle of color in the sky caused by light shining through rain or fog.

Respect: To feel or show honor.

Robber: A person who steals by using or threatening force.

Selfish: Too much concern for one's own things and little or no concern for others.

Sheep: A farm animal raised for its hair and meat.

Shepherd: A person who takes care of sheep.

Sword: A large sharp knife for fighting.

Thorn: A very hard part of a tree with a sharp point.

Thunder: The sound that follows a flash of lightning.